AF581735

Luxury Edition

The 52 Fables of Power

Verses of Dominance: Unveiling the Mysteries of Influence and Command

Tom Levy

First edition: November 2023

ISBN: 978-2-89864-007-0

Published by: 01 Web Canada

Preface

Since the dawn of time, man has sought to understand and harness power. He has gazed upon the stars, questioned nature, and delved deep into the human soul to decipher the mysteries of this intangible and omnipotent force. But what is power? Is it a gift, a curse, or a subtle art to master?

In "The 52 Fables of Power", we explore this concept through the lens of the fable, an ancient literary genre which, through its seeming simplicity, unveils the deepest truths of human existence. Each fable, inspired by the universal laws of power, portrays a specific facet of this force, shedding light on the strategies, pitfalls, triumphs, and tragedies that ensue.

These fables aren't just tales to tell; they are mirrors in which we can see our own reflections, guides that assist us in navigating the intricate maze of power. Whether read for enjoyment, enlightenment, or strategic inspiration, these narratives are designed to touch both the heart and the mind.

As our modern world appears to be increasingly saturated with power quests, manipulations, and strategies, it's vital to remember that power, in its essence, is both a sword and a shield. And like any weapon, it's essential to know how to wield it.

I thus invite you to dive into this collection, to ponder, question, and immerse yourself in the timeless lessons of these fables. Whether you seek to understand power, to gain it, or simply to contemplate it, these tales are for you.

Table des matières

In **'The 52 Fables of Power'**, tales wise and grand,
Lessons for life, secrets in every strand.
In each tale, a gem of wisdom to unfold,
Power and life, stories both new and old.

Each page paints a scene, tales stretching wide,
Musings on strength and influence, side by side.
A captivating journey through these tales fifty-two,
Power in its many forms, in light or mirrored view.

May each fable inspire, light the path ahead,
The power of mind, of heart, in the tale thread.
In these **52 Fables**, an adventure to explore,
To learn, to grow, and wisdom to implore.

1. The Young Wolf and the Ancient Lion

Deep within a forest, wild and vast,
Lived an ancient lion, a relic from the past.
Though his mane was white and his pace less spry,
He still held a regal gleam in his eye.

A young wolf, eager to claim some fame,
Arrived one day, staking his claim.
Impressed yet ambitious, the crown he did desire,
Wishing to dethrone, he stoked the fire.

"Old lion," he declared, "why do you lead?
Your time has passed, fulfill this deed.
Challenge if you must, with vigor and song,
But know that experience has made me strong."

The lion, with grace, set forth a task so clear,
"Catch the cunning hare that roams near here."
The wolf dashed forth, full of pride,
Yet the hare danced away, its escape justified.

Hours later, the wolf, defeated, withdrew,
The lion then showed what experience can do.
With swift precision, as night's sky turned black,
The hare was caught; the king had his throne back.

The forest whispered of the tale so grand,
Of the lion who, with age, still took a stand.
For wisdom and cunning will always outpace,
Raw strength and youth, in life's endless race.

Moral:

As you rise, remember the sight,

Of those above, shining bright.

Each choice you make, every stance,

Is watched, noted, given a glance.

Don't flaunt your skills or be too loud,

In a world where pride's not allowed.

Eclipsing the master, a perilous quest,

For the ambitious, it's a rigorous test.

Travel with caution, step with poise,

Hold modesty close, amidst the noise.

Respect those in lead, let them shine and glow,

To the heights of influence, you're bound to grow.

2. The Heron, the Duck, and the Vulture

By a serene pond, a lone heron stood tall,
Proud of its grandeur, looking down on all.
Every day by its side, swam a duck from days of yore,
Always offering counsel, speaking of love evermore.

From the skies above, a vulture did glare,
An old foe of the heron, watching with a vengeful stare.
One day the duck offered a plan to fish side by side,
Promising plentiful catches, with the tide.

Distrustful, the heron declined, recalling past deceit,
But the duck pressed on, with words so sweet.
Reluctantly, the heron agreed, hoping for a grand feast,
Unaware it was a trap, with the duck as the beast.

From high above, the vulture spied the unfolding snare,
Dove swiftly down, sending the duck to the open air.
Grateful, the heron invited the vulture to stay,
From foes they turned allies, facing all challenges that lay.

Moral:

A friend might betray, driven by jealousy or jest,
But a defeated enemy's gratitude can often be the best.
Don't place all bets on friendship; it can be a façade,
With a former rival by your side, loyalty's more broad.

Beware of smiling friends, for some may deceive,
By envy, they change courses and weave.
While some act on whims, even becoming despots,
An old adversary, trying to prove, can be gracious a lot.

More dangerous are friends than declared adversaries,
For from betrayed friendships come many miseries.
If you lack enemies, seek some out and make,
For they'll keep you on your toes, always awake.

3. The Fox, the Rabbit, and the Owl

In a vast, dense forest, with tall and thick trees,
A cunning fox hunted, with sharp, gleaming eyes at ease.
At every turn, he found the rabbit, nimble and plump,
Always eluding his claws with calculated jumps and lumps.

One day, the fox said to the rabbit, in false camaraderie:
"Let's search together, by the moonlight, for berries, see?"
The rabbit, wary but curious, accepted the invite,
Hoping to discern the intentions, the reason for this respite.

But the fox, master of deceit, had another scheme in play,
He wanted to lead him astray, into a trap by day.
He spoke of distant hills, of enchanted woods and tales,
Concealing his motives under charming, beguiling veils.

From his perch, the owl observed with keen sight,
Grasping the fox's motives in the pale moonlight.
Softly, he shared the sly scheme with the hare,
Who quickly escaped, leaving the fox in despair.

When the fox realized his scheme had been unveiled,
It was already too late, the rabbit had set sail.
"Deception is an art," thought the fox in dismay,
"But against a watchful observer, I always lose my way."

Moral:

In mystery keep your deeds tight,

Let ambiguity be your guiding light.

When those around seek to discern,

Let the smokescreen make them yearn.

For if your goal remains concealed,

None can surpass you or take the lead.

And when they finally see the truth clear,

You'll have already taken to the frontier.

Conceal your aims, but know the wise eye,

Sees through illusions, piercing the lie.

In the art of deceit, vigilance is the key,

For every step forward hides a reality unseen.

4. The Sparrow, the Crow, and the Dove

In the hollow of an old oak, the birds convened,
To discuss a riddle that had them all intrigued.
The sparrow, lively and chatty, chirped away,
Hoping with his tales, the echoes he'd sway.

The crow, black and imposing, spoke with aplomb,
Yet his many words seemed to lack substance and charm.
He strung words together, aiming to dominate all,
But with his verbose speech, he made their interest fall.

Then, the dove, softly, sang a calm and serene tune,
Each word chosen, each note felt like a boon.
Her brief speech, pure and filled with finesse,
Left a deep echo, touching the soul with tenderness.

The audience, enchanted, hung on every phrase,
Her innate grace guided them, like wind guides bird's ways.
They were mesmerized, captivated by her eloquence,
Every word weighed, every silence held significance.

Moral:

Speak little, but aptly, a sign of true might,

Too many words harm, diminishing the light.

Choose words with care, and measure their space,

In moderation, true elegance takes its place.

Chatter makes the mind all too mundane,

Silence, on the other hand, has a charming domain.

Remain elusive, keep some mystery intact,

Say too much, and you risk being detracted.

The wise know to preserve their speech,

For in talking too much, damage is within reach.

5. The Swan, the Carp, and the Crayfish

In the heart of a clear pond, the Swan thrived with flair,
Envied by all the bank's dwellers for its beauty so rare.
White as snow, noble in its stance,
Each ripple it made was like a graceful dance.

The Carp, with envious green eyes, observed this sight,
Dreaming of praises, wishing to be in the limelight.
Together with the Crayfish, a partner insincere,
They hatched a plot, in the shadow of the ferns near.

They whispered of a pearl, allegedly stolen away,
Which the Swan, they claimed, had hidden in its bay.
But the Swan, ever upright, rose above these lies,
Proving its innocence to all, its truth clear in the skies.

The owl, with piercing eyes, saw through their deceit,
Carp and Crayfish were chased away, their scheme in defeat.
The Swan, majestic, resumed its gentle sway,
Against slander, its grandeur had carried the day.

Moral:

Your reputation is what always precedes your act,
Against slander, it serves as your protective pact.
In a world where envy wears the crown,
Hold your name dear, it's your renown.

Reputation is a gleaming golden crown,
The key to power, a treasure renowned.
If kept untarnished, you'll be praised so high,
But blemished, it will leave you alone to sigh.

Guard it as your most precious asset, so true,
For losing it is a step towards your undoing, too.
And if you must confront a foe,
Strike at his reputation, deal that blow.

Then step back, and watch the crowd react,
For a tarnished name is hard to redact.

6. The Peacock and the Mole

In the heart of the forest, under a radiant sky,
The Peacock shimmered, spreading his feathers high.
At dawn, his brilliance dazzled without defeat,
Capturing every gaze, he ruled the festive beat.

He danced and sang, overshadowing the wild,
With his majesty, he wore the crown, ever beguiled.
Drawn to his light, they gathered near,
Admiring in silence, but with a touch of envy, clear.

The Mole, discreet, worked in the shadow's might,
Invisible and humble, but she held a dream so tight.
One day, inspired by the Peacock and his fame,
She decided to emerge, seeking her own name.

She planted flowers, creating an underground grove,
Inviting all the animals to an endless feast trove.
Soon, her home became a favored gathering place,
Her perseverance and passion put her in the grace.

For even though everyone has their own light to display,
With determination, everyone can shine in their own way.
The Peacock had his feathers, the Mole her magical glen,
Each in their own way, in the forest, had made their den.

Moral:

In the world's theater, where the eye is king,

Only the one seen in the spotlight does sing.

Don't be a shadow, but a flame in the night,

For only brilliance attracts where gray does smite.

Do not settle for mere existence, be the beacon afar,

Draw attention, shine, be the star, even in the darkest hour.

For in this vast world, where all is transient and sheer,

Only the one capturing gazes writes their story clear.

7. The Raven and the Sparrows

Atop a high branch, the Raven took its stance,
Watching the Sparrows busy in their dance.
They gathered seeds, tirelessly, without end,
While the Raven showed no strain or bend.

"Why not help me out?" he asked one day,
"I'm building a grand nest, for all birds to stay."
The Sparrows, naive and trusting, accepted the bid,
Thinking of a shelter for all, like a protective lid.

Day by day, they brought twigs and moss,
While the Raven from its perch, with a toss,
Shouted commands, orders, and advice too,
Always demanding, yet never a hand did he put to.

The nest was finally done, grand and wide,
The Sparrows, worn out, expected pride.
But the Raven declared, "See what I have made!
A palace for birds, by my sole crusade!"

Other birds, in awe, praised the Raven high,
Forgetting those who truly bore the supply.
The Sparrows, bitter and sad, stayed mute,
Realizing too late the lesson and its root.

Moral:

In the shadows of talents, make your stride,

Drawing from their wisdom, become the guide.

Save your steps, let others pave the way,

But be at the forefront, come the day of pay.

Let their toil become the pillar of your seat,

For at the top, it's you the glory will greet.

Remember well this motto in every task,

From others' hands benefit, while in glory you bask.

8. The Fox and the Boar

In a vast forest, a cunning Fox did reside,
Always on the lookout for a scheme well-devised.
The Boar, stout and proud, lived there too,
None dared to challenge him through.

The Fox, wanting the forest's rule,
Couldn't face the Boar, given his famed cool.
Yet he didn't despair, knowing that wit,
Often trumps a direct and fierce hit.

He invited the Boar to a distant glade,
Promising a feast, a sudden accolade.
The Boar, curious, followed the Fox in trust,
Unaware he was entering a dance of thrust.

For the ground chosen by the cunning creature,
Was littered with traps, far from discreet in nature.
The Boar found himself caught, left to fate,
The Fox had planned it all, with calculated bait.

Victorious, the Fox said, "In this vast wood stretch,
Wit and intellect outweigh raw strength in each sketch."
The Boar, trapped, learned the lesson that day,
That the battleground can decide who will sway.

Moral:

With cunning and strategy, take the lead,

Draw in the foe, make yourself the creed.

When he forsakes his game for yours instead,

You hold the cards, while his chances dreadfully shed.

Pushing him to act, you pull the string,

He dances to your tune, under your wing.

Lure with promises, a vision of boon,

For he who controls the game, holds the moon.

When you pick the battle's place,

You've already secured half the winning base.

9. The Dove and the Mantis

In a blooming garden, the Mantis did proclaim,
With a voice so sure, she alone was the dame.
"Listen, my friends, under sky and breeze,
My word is the light, your only appease."

But despite her eloquent speeches in the air,
Few felt at ease, for in shadows, she'd stare.
With a hidden hunger, she'd set her traps,
In the slender grass, her prey she'd perhaps.

Not far, a Dove, embodiment of grace,
Rarely spoke, but love was her base.
Every day, she'd offer a wounded bird's plight,
The shelter of her wings, never boasting her might.

The garden's inhabitants watched the pair,
The Mantis with her words, the Dove's silent care.
They saw clearly, by an unspoken accord,
That genuine deeds outweigh the spoken word.

The Mantis, alone, without a friend to call,
The Dove was praised, for her kindness enthralled.
Without a word, she'd touched many a heart,
For her actions spoke louder than tales from the start.

Moral:

In quietness lies a strength without show,

Where loud cries only brew sorrow and woe.

Actions, in silence, speak far louder than speech,

For leading by example is the truest reach.

Instead of preaching, let time weave its dance,

For lived examples remain in minds at a glance.

Gentle persuasion stands firmer and wise,

Than the noisy turmoil of fleeting skies.

Deeds have a voice louder than any phrase,

They resonate in hearts, long after the blaze.

10. The Peacock and the Raven

In a distant forest, a Peacock shone with a dazzling hue,
Its radiant feathers brought envy in more than a few.
Apart, a Raven, with dark feathers, lamented its fate,
Its life filled with misfortune, pain, and regret, it did state.

One day, out of pity, the Peacock came near,
Hoping with its luck, to bring the Raven some cheer.
But instead of light, darkness began to grow,
The Raven's misfortune seemed to rub off, it did show.

First, the Peacock lost a few of its feathers, as they flew,
Then, animals avoided it, without feeling askew.
The forest realized that misfortune can spread,
It's best to stay away from souls with heavy hearts of lead.

For trying to save a drowning soul, might pull you in too,
Sometimes it's wiser to preserve oneself and keep your hue.

Moral:

Others' misfortune might become your sorrow,
Avoid the contagious, seek a brighter tomorrow.
With light hearts, with souls so free,
For in their company, life feels like glee.

Avoid the dark auras, those spirits so bleak,
For another's misfortune might be the weakness you seek.
In trying to save a soul caught in despair,
You might sink too, caught unaware.

The unlucky ones bring storms and strife,
Around them whirlwinds rife.
Seek the light, those who shine so bright,
For by their side, days are filled with delight.

11. The Spring and the Villagers

In the heart of the village, a crystal-clear spring,
Generous every day, its water a refreshing thing.
But as time went by, its virtue was overlooked,
Until one day its true value was again booked.

A village sage, who'd seen arid lands,
Spoke of places without water, where life stands.
"Without our spring, where would we be, my friends?
Like flowers without rain, withering at both ends."

Touched by these words, the villagers convened,
They chose to celebrate the spring, it was deemed.
They planted flowers around, built a small wall,
A place of gratitude, a festive secret hall.

Each year, a festivity in its honor took place,
To remind all of its value, its fervor, its grace.
The spring, more than water, was their life's core,
They learned to cherish it, forevermore.

Moral:

By giving, by serving, by always being near,
You make yourself essential, you won't be in the rear.
Be like that spring, valuable in each deed,
And others around will see you as their need.

To keep your glow, be the guiding star,
That everyone seeks, no matter how far.
Nurture your knowledge, your unique flair,
For the more they rely on you, the greater your share.

Never give everything, keep some mysteries alive,
For in the shadows, your true light will thrive.
Let them never move forward without your lead,
For that's how your freedom will proceed.

12. The Fox and the Crow

In a dense forest, the Crow, usually so miserly,
Found some cheese, flaunting it so brightly.
The Fox, enticed, saw an unparalleled chance,
Said, "Dear Crow, your find enchants me at a glance.

I'm hungry, indeed, but I have a suggestion to make:
My berries for your cheese, a fair exchange for both our sake.
Thus, with fairness, we both get a deserving share,
A balanced trade, an act so rare and square.

The Crow, initially wary, eyed the gleaming berries,
And the genuine face of the Fox, without any trickeries.
He agreed to the offer, and they both enjoyed a just feast,
Demonstrating mutual trust, without the least deceit released.

But as the Crow departed, pleased with the swap,
The Fox, grinning, thought, "Today, I was atop.
Today I was true; tomorrow I might deceive.
Honesty opens doors, that cunning can't achieve."

Moral:

A genuine act softens many a gaze,
Builds bridges, drives away the dark haze.
But honesty, when cleverly played,
Becomes a concealed blade, subtly displayed.

In guile, feigned sincerity paves the way,
A truthful act might sometimes hide hefty pay.
Like the Trojan Horse with its hidden aims,
Apparent honesty can be the master of games.

By extending a hand, distrust is lulled,
Under the veil of genuineness, schemes are culled.
When trust is drawn by a presented gift,
In the shadow of truth, plans may shift.

13. The Cat and the Mouse in Business

Under the moonlight, a Mouse emerged from its hide,
Seeking food, unaware of the peril that might coincide.
The Cat, a silent shadow, eyed his fleeting meal,
But rather than pounce, a cunning plan made him feel real.

"Little Mouse," he whispered, "instead of being my bite,
Why not combine our skills and make things right?
I've seen you find where man hides his treasures best,
I've watched you steal cheeses, passing every test."

The Mouse, wary, retorted, "What if you betray the scheme?
The moment I turn, your claws might make me scream."
"If I consume you, I'd lose a perpetual delight,
But in partnership, cheeses would be a regular sight."

Grasping the feline's motive, and not his empathy,
The Mouse sealed their pact, forming an unlikely fraternity.
From this rare tandem, a strategic friendship did emerge,
Each reaping benefits, as moonbeams cast their surge.

Moral:

In the vast theater of life, acts shine and then fade,
Generous gestures sometimes fall like stars from the glade.
But beware the light that's dazzling but brief,
For tomorrow it might die, leaving behind a bitter grief.

Mutual interest, on the other hand, is an enduring flame,
Illuminating paths, giving rise to alliances of fame.
In this changing world, where everything fast-forwards and flies,
Shared interest is an anchor, a foundation, the ultimate prize.

Seek to establish bonds of interest and share,
For mutual gain is a solid adhesive, defying wear and tear.
When two hands clasp, driven by a common aim,
They build sturdy bridges, warding off every pain

14. The Fox, the Magpie, and the Raven

In a shadowy woodland, Fox and Magpie lived side by side.
Both desired the seat upon which the Raven did preside.
"The essence of might, is in the knowledge we keep.
Let's observe, let's uncover, and the throne we shall reap."

Dazzled, the Magpie flew, listened, and reported back,
While the cunning Fox analyzed every tidbit and track.
At the birds' feasts, he would keenly listen,
Amassing secrets, expanding his vision.

The Magpie, ever so chatty, mentioned the Fox,
Oblivious that he too was skilled in such talks.
The Raven, being alerted, expressed gratitude to the Fox,
Yet with a cunning grin, sent him away to the distant docks

"Espionage," he said, "is a perilous trade.
Even the craftiest can fall victim to their own charade."

Moral:

Behind honeyed words may lurk a spy,

Using trust as a ladder to aim high.

Knowledge can indeed be a significant boon,

But the art of spying requires a subtle tune.

Keep your gaze sharp and move with discretion,

For those who learn too much might reveal their own confession.

In the quiet dance of shadows and light,

Each exposed secret shines ever so bright.

But beware the insatiable hunger for knowledge,

It can darken every moment, leaving one on the edge.

For in desiring too much, one invites strife,

And by one's own doing, risks a fall in life.

15. The Lion and the Snake

In the heart of the savannah, a Lion, proud and grand,
Had built an empire, vast and spanning the land.
All animals quivered at his golden mane's sight,
Except for a Snake, stealthy, challenging without fright.

One day, the Snake bit one of the Lion's young,
Inflicting brief pain, like a bell that'd been rung.
Enraged, the Lion sought to punish this meddler,
But roared and left the Snake unfettered.

Grateful for his luck, the Snake hid in the shade,
Patiently waiting for the Lion to make a grave charade.
And on a night when the Lion slept without a care,
The Snake struck, injecting venom in the air.

The savannah was in shock, seeing the king wane,
While the Snake laughed, readying to reign.
Where the Lion had shown mercy and lenience,
The Snake had chosen madness and defiance.

Moral:

When an enemy rises, strong and tall,
Do not leave them any room at all.
For embers left beneath the ash,
Might flare up again, in a dangerous flash.

Great leaders of old, etched in tales,
Knew that threats must meet their fails.
Give them a chance, and they'll return,
Stronger, craftier, ready to churn.

Don't settle for half-won battles and truce,
For mercy often opens doors of misuse.
Eliminate the danger, heart and soul,
Thus, you'll ensure a future without a toll.

16. The Diamond and the Pebble

On a golden beach, two stones did speak,
One shone brightly, the other seemed weak.
The Diamond, rare and precious, was much desired,
The Pebble, plain and dull, had nothing admired.

"Why do humans chase after you with so much zeal?"
Asked the Pebble, with a heart that was real.
"I'm rare," replied the Diamond with a superior vibe,
"My sparkle brings joy, in me, they imbibe."

But as time passed, the beach began to shift,
The Pebble became rare, taken by tides and time's drift.
Visitors sought this stone for their games and glee,
Its newfound rarity made it shine brightly, you see.

The Diamond, always locked away, started losing its glow,
For what's ever-present often becomes mundane, as we know.
The Pebble, by its absence, became the shore's prized part,
Proving value comes from rarity, not just age or art.

Moral:

Sometimes, in the shadows, it's best to stay,

For what's rare is desired, in an unending way.

Constant presence turns precious to plain,

But absence magnifies allure, that's the main gain.

If among birds, you wish to shine and gleam,

You must know when to fade, to be highly esteemed.

For he who knows when to step back and be rare,

Will return as a king, with many a stare.

Value isn't measured by hours you're around,

But in mystery, surprise, and the wait that's unbound.

Practice absence, be the shooting star's glance,

For by making yourself scarce, your brilliance will enhance.

17. The Fox and the Chameleon

In a thick, green forest, vast and immense,
The Fox, with pride, maintained his cadence.
Beside him walked a Chameleon ever-changing,
Shifting its hues, its colors constantly rearranging.

"Why this routine, this path every day?",
Asked the Chameleon, observing with a gaze to display.
The Fox, with a smile, revealed his game:
"A set path simplifies my aim."

The Chameleon, adept in surprise and adaptability,
Retorted: "In me, there's no fixed ability.
No eye can predict the hue I'll embrace,
Like a living riddle, I enjoy leaving them off-base."

One morning, a hunter, seeking game to ensnare,
Knowing the Fox's path, set a trap with care.
The Fox, by habit, fell into it without any dread,
While the Chameleon evaded the threat overhead.

Moral:

In life's dance, habits tend to lead,

We follow set paths, in which we find creed.

But one who constantly changes, remaining unpredictable,

Sows doubt and confusion, becoming invincible.

Just when you think you've understood, they change the play,

Without rhyme or reason, purely introspective sway.

People around ponder, seeking some clue,

Exhausted, they fear what next they might do.

Unpredictability is a weapon, an endless enigma,

It bestows power, an aura of infinite charisma.

For in the unknown, man often feels fright,

So be that mysterious puzzle, and control their plight.

18. The Eagle and the Dove

Atop a high cliff, it sat in might,
The Eagle watching for a prey to sight.
Below, the Dove frolicked in mirth,
Singing in the woods, with carefree worth.

One day, driven by hunger's urge,
Towards the gentle creature, the Eagle wanted to surge.
But alerted by friends, the Dove was made aware,
She darted through the trees, escaping the snare.

Desolate on his perch, the Eagle realized,
That not everything under the sky can be prized.
The Dove, in her grace, celebrated camaraderie,
For in nature, mutual aid is the strongest armory.

Moral:

Isolation may seem like power in one's course,

But in togetherness, we find the true source.

In life's jungle, threats around each bend,

Everyone seeks shelter, from the harm that might send.

Without the world's echo, news becomes scarce,

One becomes an easy target, with no one to parley or converse.

For distancing from all can birth suspicions, and one becomes aloof,

Isolation casts shadows, and maybe secrets under the roof.

Better then to walk amidst the bustling crowd,

To blend in, to dance, seeking bonds aloud.

The crowd acts as a shield, warding off a foe,

Within it, we hide and allies we get to know.

19. The Lion and the Porcupine

The Lion, king of the savanna, took pride in his reign,
Each day showcasing his might, without any restrain.
One day, he met a creature he'd never seen in due,
A Porcupine, bristling with quills, standing in the avenue.

Seeing an opportunity to display his grand stature,
The Lion approached, roaring with rapture.
He thought he'd make a meal of this tiny creature at bay,
But some won't back down, even to a king's dismay.

The Porcupine curled up, his quills at the ready,
Repelling every attack, keeping steady.
The Lion, frustrated and injured, retreated in shame,
He had underestimated his opponent, to his own blame.

Moral:

In life's grand ball, watch where you step and advance,
For some won't forgive a wrongful dance.
If by mistake you tread on another's shoe without care,
Beware of shadows, as some may bear betrayal rare.

Behind each mask lies a story, a soul,
And what seems soft might have a fiery role.
The wolf might dress as a lamb, so sly and discreet,
Mistreat the wrong one, and darkness you'll meet.

Choose your battles wisely, weigh each move you cast,
For a careless offense can leave a lasting blast.
In the world's waltz, each step must be wise and free,
For one wrong move, and the dance turns into a spree.

20. The Cat and the Two Sparrows

In the heart of a clearing, two sparrows sang,
One praising the daylight, the other the night's tang.
Leon, with a clear voice, exalted the day's glow,
While Rene, of the night, its mysteries did he show.

From this rivalry, the forest split in two ways,
But Whiskers, a cunning cat, danced in both plays.
From Leon, he embraced the daytime song,
From Rene, he appreciated the night's song all along.

Curious animals, to Whiskers they all came,
Seeking the harmony that only his song could claim.
Whiskers, from their feud, reaped a benefit so neat,
Gathering from each bird, what made his joy complete.

Leon and Rene, in their struggle so consumed,
Saw their influence gradually get doomed.
Whiskers, enriched by both arts, shone so bright,
Showing that between two sides, the middle's just right.

Moral:

Amid conflicts, stay on the middle line,
Pledge allegiance to no flag, to no sign.
For he who ties himself to a cause loses his freedom to play,
While the independent enjoys a diverse array.

By keeping your distance, you become the night's beacon,
All eyes turn to you, seeking a glow, a reason.
Pit one against another, with skill and grace,
For mastering the strings, you hold the ace.

To lead the dance, to set the pace,
For the independent, in his nuance, finds his space.

21. The Crafty Fisherman and the Merchant

In the heart of a village where the market did shine,
Each weekend, crowds would gather, forming a line.
Erwan, a boastful merchant, draped in cunning and flair,
His fame grew rapidly, and so did his air.

Leon, the clever fisherman, made his entrance grand,
With a basket heavy, full of fish from the land.
"Erwan", he whispered, "I need a favor, you see,
Could you, with your skills, sell this catch for me?"

With a proud smile, Erwan did agree,
"I'll show you, my friend, how it's done with glee!"
The crowd gathered around, each fish was sold fast,
For Erwan proclaimed a deal, that was unsurpassed.

But when the time came to share the golden gain,
Leon, with mischief, revealed his clever brain.
"For your invaluable help, this fish I bestow to thee,
While for myself, dear Erwan, I keep the golden spree."

The merchant stood there, his vanity wounded deep,
While the fisherman went on, his earnings to keep.
Sometimes, humility over cunning does win,
And silence, against boasting, is the best way in.

Moral:

In the dance of minds, where everyone seeks the light,

The desire to be wise can sometimes make us slip from the right.

For he who rises, might sometimes fall from the sky,

But he who stays silent, watches every mistake go by.

Let your neighbor believe he's the cleverest one,

Let him bask in his own illusory sun.

For man, in his vanity, dreams sweet dreams so wrong,

Thinking he's the wise one, not seeing the shadow so long.

The subtle game is to pretend to be a fool,

For under the humble mask, cunning gets its fuel.

Let him think he's cunning, sharp, and aware,

Meanwhile, in silence, chart your path without a care.

22. The Prideful King and the Wise Warrior

Atop a high and majestic mountain peak,
Alden ruled, with everything seemingly at his beck.
His palace shimmered, in gold and gem's gleam,
Echoing his pride, without limit or seam.

From a distant horizon, Caelan came into view,
A hero of old tales, with a challenge anew.
The battle was fierce as they stood toe to toe,
Every strike from Alden, Caelan did foreknow.

"King Alden," said Caelan, "your pride does betray.
Acknowledge your mistake or your reign ends today."
But Alden, in his pride, couldn't yield the day,
And with a decisive blow, Caelan swept him away.

The court in silence, saw their king meet the ground,
Caelan, noble and wise, refused the crown to be found.
The lesson was clear, for those who did stay,
Unrestrained pride will, one day, lead you astray.

Moral:

In life's battlefield, where egos do clash,

Sometimes we're cornered, in a moment so rash.

When defeat looms large, without any sway,

Isn't it wiser to reconsider one's way?

Don't pursue the fight from mere pride alone,

For timely surrender has a beauty of its own.

To yield brings a moment of serene grace,

To heal, reflect, and regain one's place.

Your opponent expects your downfall, your defeat,

But by raising the white flag, you can turn the heat.

Your submission might pique their keen interest,

And in their victory, a vulnerability might manifest.

For to surrender is not to show you're weak,

It's an art, a strategy, a ploy unique.

Giving up, far more than a bitter end,

Is a tool of power, a sincere tactic to commend.

23. The Gardener and the Sun

In the heart of a village of unmatched peace,
Théobald, the gardener, dreamt without cease.
He envisioned his garden, in flowers aglow,
Scattering seeds far and wide, letting them blow.

But the Sun, from its golden throne high,
Looked upon Théobald with a questioning eye.
Descending to Earth, in a man's guise it came,
Questioning the gardener's relentless aim.

"Why sow so widely, without much thought?
Do you not see, by scattering, you gain naught?"
Théobald, taken aback, began to ponder,
"I thought by sowing more, my wealth would grow fonder."

The Sun, gently, made him see the light,
"Choose your lands, focus, and all will be right.
Don't sow to the wind, be like water with a plan,
For in the depths, treasures hide, waiting for a man."

Théobald heeded, refining his stance,
To chosen plants, he gave his full expanse.
The village marveled, at such wondrous view,
For quality, over quantity, had its due.

Moral:

Deep in the mountain's heart, a secret does dwell,

Seeking gold on the surface is to choose the rose's smell,

Ignoring its roots, its true story to tell,

Fleeting beauty reigns, while treasures in shadows swell.

Dive deep, where truths are concealed,

Don't settle for what's easily revealed.

Rich veins lie where strength is sealed,

Intensity shines, when breadth has been repealed.

Don't scatter like a leaf in the wind's dance,

Focus, be like water, flow with nuance.

Find a mentor, a nurturing expanse,

A generous stream, for a lasting chance.

For true power lies in depth's embrace,

Where gold is pure, and hearts hold no trace.

Seek your core, your strength, your grace,

And therein, you'll find happiness' base.

24. The Peacock and the Nightingale

In Leonidas' palace, where the court comes alive,
Creatures seek favor, in numbers they thrive.
Pristus the peacock, dons his radiant feathers bright,
While Melodia, the discreet, watches from a distant sight.

Pristus, in pride, parades his splendid array,
Each step, each motion, an artful display.
He knows how to praise, to flatter without a right,
Yet within him, an emptiness, a vanity too trite.

Melodia, from her perch, sings in hushed refrain,
Her voice, a gentle melody, a subtle disdain.
She doesn't flatter, but observes the scene,
And offers, in due time, wisdom that's serene.

Confronted with a quandary, Leonidas ponders deep,
Pristus steps forward, but his words seem hollow and cheap.
Melodia, with a melody gentle yet profound,
Guides the king with insight, drawing him around.

The nightingale's voice, so pure and so fine,
Eclipses the peacock, with its darkened line.
Pristus, despite his glimmering, splendid guise,
Before true wisdom, bows down and complies.

Moral:

In the arena of courts, where power takes its stance,
The courtier dances, between shadow and chance.
He moves covertly, feigning innocence and grace,
Mastering the art of ambiguity, where the strong leave their trace.

Flatter the mighty, but never overdo,
Bow before him, yet keep mysteries in view.
Rule the weaker, with quiet dominance and tact,
With courtesy, stand firm, never retract.

In this delicate game, where strategy is key,
One must read the rules, know each ally's decree.
For he who is aware, and never does forget,
Will see doors open, his power set.

Thus, if you aim for the highest ascent,
Observe, listen, and always be intent.
For in the court, where power is the trend,
Only the skilled courtier knows the echo's end.

25. The Lion and the Chameleon

In a vast forest, beneath the azure sky,
Leo, the lion, had earned his royal title high.
Proud of his strength, his echoing roar,
He reminded every beast of his rank, evermore.

But in these woods, Cal, the discreet chameleon,
Shifted his hues, mastering the art of deception.
Avoiding peril, he watched without tension,
Learning from others, with utmost discretion.

When drought struck the region, leaving streams dry,
All were lost, fearing devastation nigh.
Leo, in arrogance, sought to take command,
Claiming all, he spread chaos across the land.

Yet Cal, the subtle, charted another course,
Blending with the beasts, he understood the source.
Proposing a plan, ensuring life would advance,
His cunning worked, the forest took a chance.

Grateful gazes turned to Cal, admiration clear,
Leo, now dethroned, finally began to hear:
Brute strength alone doesn't pave every course,
Subtle power, too, has its own driving force.

Moral:

In life's grand theater, under blazing lights,
Don't merely cast a shadow of prevailing trite.
Carve your unique role, enchantingly bright,
Leaving behind the whispers of the spite.

Don't let the masses sculpt your face,
Nor past echoes chart your trace.
Master of your image, crafting illusions in space,
Resist the chains, every cage you'll displace.

Strike high and hard, with a spectacular deed,
Make an indelible mark, with a unique creed.
Your power will grow, like sunlight indeed,
And your stature, like the North Star, will lead.

26. The Owl and the Rat

In the heart of the city, two figures arise,
One, a discerning owl, the other a rat full of disguise.
Oscar, with wisdom, leads and unifies,
While Hector, cunning, plays with the ties.

When a famine struck the land,
Granaries ran low, causing despair to expand.
Oscar, behind the scenes, saw the plot firsthand,
And used Hector, who couldn't understand the planned.

He hinted to the rat, with an indifferent tone,
To hoard grains, possibly for selling them alone.
Hector, eyes gleaming, sensing a growth zone,
Jumped into action, unaware of the impending dethrone.

Oscar, meanwhile, stayed aside,
Watching the rat hoard, increasing his stride.
When the city suffered from the divide,
He pointed at Hector, blaming him for the downside.

The city, outraged, punished the greedy rat,
Unaware of his deals, he was left alone and flat.
Oscar, unshaken, received praises and admiring chats,
Without lifting a finger, his reputation remained intact.

For in this tale, cunning had its say,
Act behind the curtains, let others face the dismay.

Moral:

In the world's grand theater with its plays,

Where deceit often takes the front phase,

Be the beacon that never sways,

The unwavering soul, that never betrays.

Rise high, a paragon of integrity,

Away from the lows and betrayals of society.

For in the shadows, traps lay heavily,

Ensure you remain beyond the reach of duplicity.

Yet in this dance, be sharp and smart,

Use others to face the riskier part.

Let them forge ahead, seeking your chart,

While you stay back, smooth, free of the art.

Thus, in the game of power and trust,

You remain clean, above all, and just.

27. The Enigmatic Prophet

In a realm of disputes and squabbles,
Alaric emerges, eluding all gazes and troubles.
Dressed in dazzling garments that catch the eye,
His voice resonates, dismissing every lie.

He speaks of a land where all would be calm,
Where peace would rule, keeping away every harm.
Vague words, soft promises, bright and vast,
Crowds rush in, spirits move fast.

Mystical gatherings, grand in their might,
Devotees in a trance, in a somber light.
To prove their faith, offerings they make,
There, Alaric sits, god-like, for everyone's sake.

Warriors, lords, all come to his side,
Leaving behind old banners, with nothing to hide.
Power in these lands shifts to his space,
This enigmatic prophet takes his rightful place.

But to doubt him was to risk being cast away,
For in his aura, doubt was mere child's play.
Untouchable, ghostly he appeared to be,
In his vague promises, the kingdom found glee.

His power grew, day by day,
His words charmed, velvety in every way.
No sign of weakness, no sign of bend,
Alaric shone, his happiness had no end.

Doubts were quietly set aside,
Before the prophet, reverence couldn't hide.
In the realm, his command was undisputed,
With faith and words, his stature was saluted

Moral:

In the vast universe of the human soul,

Seek grounding, a chaining light's goal.

To you, leader, knowing this deep desire,

Offer a star, a dream that never does tire.

Vague words, but shining with promise so clear,

Float in the air, fill their despair here.

No need for logic, nor for reasoning true,

Passion alone makes people's hearts renew.

Offer them rituals, sacred gestures and more,

Songs, dances, secrets galore.

Ask for sacrifice, devotion, blind trust,

For in this surrender, your power grows, just and robust.

For man, at his core, seeks to believe,

Offer him a cult, and watch your glory achieve.

28. Elenor's Odyssey

Nestled among the mountains, Elenor dwelled,
A pride of a peaceful village, as tales tell.
Yet beyond the peaks, her heart yearned to roam,
To explore the uncharted, to make the unknown known
.
Villagers spoke of beasts, and terrors that bind,
Of cursed summits, and horrors they'd find.
But in Elenor, a daring flame did burn,
Urging her forward at every turn.

One day, her journey she finally began,
Facing perils, her bravery ran.
Wolves, rivers, cliffs to scale,
Nothing could her determination derail.

Reaching the peak, the vista unfurled,
A wondrous unknown world she beheld.
No monsters, just the beauty of a place,
Hidden by myths from their embrace.

Returning home, her feats they praised,
For her bravery and courage, voices were raised.
She'd proven, with passion and quest so grand,
Beyond the fears, the horizon did stand.

Moral:

When uncertainty seeps into your soul,

Don't act if doubts take their toll.

For hesitation is a weight to bear,

Stifling dreams, making one forgo the dare.

But if boldness in you takes the lead,

March forth, let nothing impede.

For even if you stumble along the way,

It's the bold who'll hold sway.

Right your wrongs with courage anew,

Face storms with resolve, through and through.

The one who dares is the one we laud,

While the timid lingers, and is often flawed.

29. Tristan's Path

In a distant land, Tristan, young and driven,
Dreamed of a grand bridge, under the heavens given.
Linking two cities, once divided by stream,
He saw trade flourish, bridging a dream.

Many laughed at his vision, deemed it wild,
But Tristan, unyielding, was never defiled.
He studied bridges from lands afar,
Consulted experts, sketched every bar.

With budget in hand, and timeline set tight,
He foresaw every challenge, every plight.
Storms did rage, materials went scarce,
Conflicts arose, but he never lost his course.

For, armed with a plan, and vision so true,
He overcame every hurdle, every issue.
And the day the bridge connected both shores,
All marveled at its strength, its forever doors.

Those who had scoffed, now stood in awe,
But Tristan, humbly, from afar did draw.
Knowing his success, more than a skilled hand,
Came from a distant vision, and a plan so grand.

Moral:

In fate's intricate play, all is in flux,

Every step, every choice, leads to what's next.

Anticipate the pitfalls, every twist and bend,

So future surprises won't upend.

Consider the consequences, rising barriers so,

The whims of fate, that might overthrow.

Chart your path, with thought and care,

Lest you face bitter despair.

Don't be caught off guard, by mid-journey strife,

For if all's accounted for, you'll thrive in life.

Steer fortune with finesse and craft,

So it becomes an ally, not a draught.

Have a vision, stretching far and wide,

For he who sees afar, will in triumph reside.

And always remember, in every situation,

In foresight lies the solution.

30. The Artist and the Statue

In a peaceful hamlet, an artist did shine,
For his wondrous works that all deemed divine.
One day, with immense pride, he did show,
A woman carved from stone, seemingly aglow.

The villagers, awestruck by this feat so rare,
Praised: "Such elegance, beyond compare!"
"In her was concealed," he spoke with grace,
"I merely removed all that was out of place."

But behind his words, a secret lay concealed,
Months of toil that he never revealed.
Drafts, mistakes, and sleepless nights,
To breathe life into stone, he faced countless plights.

Yet this struggle, this sweat, he never did show,
For the work should speak, not the efforts below.
And in this discretion, his legend did grow,
The genius in the shadows, the magic's afterglow.

Moral:

In the shadow of effort, hide your strain,

Make each action appear free from pain.

Let your deeds shine, light and free,

Conceal the scars, the chains unseen.

For the world admires grace and ease,

Not the sweat, nor the tenacious pleas.

Let them believe, to you, it's all child's play,

That you achieve more, without a hint of dismay.

Never reveal your secret tricks and means,

For they could become double-edged screens.

In silence, keep your strategies so tight,

Let them marvel, in the magic of your might.

31. The Shepherd and the Wolves

In a distant village, a shepherd did reside,
Two fields of white sheep, by his side did bide.
Of wolves, he would tell, attacking night and day,
He pleaded for help, but found little to sway.

The villagers feared these wild beasts,
And ignored his cries, his unending feasts.
The shepherd pondered, then an idea did strike,
A cunning ruse, born from a mind so alike.

"Let's split the flocks," he announced one day,
"One with strong traps, the other in open lay.
Choose your fields wisely, think of your sheep,
For danger, my friends, does always creep."

Towards the protected field, the villagers did rush,
But the shepherd just smiled, in a silent hush.
Most wolves, in truth, had already fled,
The trap, thus, was a folly misled.

Whichever they chose, he'd be in gain,
Rent for safety, or fewer sheep to maintain.
Such is the cunning of those who know how to play,
With people's fears, leading them astray.

Moral:

In the game of illusion, the trick's well concealed,

When the victim believes, they've themselves appealed.

Thinking they control the flow and the events,

They dance along, to your elegant intents.

Offer them pathways, but all lead to thee,

Between two evils chosen, the trap is always free.

Whether they turn left, or maybe to the right,

It's your game that wins, your victory so tight.

For the greatest trick, in the art of deceit,

Is making others believe, they're in the driver's seat.

But when they make a choice, it's you who've won the day,

Caught in your web, they can't break away.

32. The Storyteller and the King

In a far-off realm, Alaric's fame did sound,
A bard of golden tone, in dreams he was crowned.
From his mouth flowed tales both old and new,
Holding every ear, to the skies they'd bid adieu.

The king, intrigued by this man of fame,
Invited him to court, seeking his rare flame.
"Tell me," he commanded, "a story that never ends,
Where mountains touch stars, and rivers of gold wend."

Enthralled, the monarch forgot his woes,
The conspiracies, famine, the threats from foes.
Only the universe, painted by the storyteller, mattered,
In this vibrant tableau, the king's thoughts were scattered.

"Stay by my side," the ruler did decide,
"And every day, with your art, our spirits you'll guide."
Alaric, within these walls, became the palace's voice,
Entertaining, influencing, altering at his choice.

For beyond the laughter, his words were keys,
Unlocking hidden doors, forgotten truths with ease.
Thus, from humble subject to elevated throne,
All were lost, delighted, in his dreamt-up zone.

Moral:

In the shadow of truth, one might hide away,
Avoiding its stark reflection, which may dismay.
Don't point at what others conceal,
For from disappointment, anger may reveal.

Life, cold and harsh, a constant test,
Seeks those who portray it with a comforting vest.
Like a gentle mirage in stark desolation,
They draw souls close, offering consolation.

To charm the hearts, appease the mind's quest,
Is to hold in one's hands a power manifest.
For in the gentle tale, where dreams take their space,
The people find shelter, and reality does erase.

33. The Merchant and the Prince

In a city of old, Rael, a shrewd trader,
Mastered crafty ploys with all of nature.
Yet Prince Ezar, proud and unwavering,
Remained untouched by deals or flattering.

Undeterred, Rael sought the secret reason,
For the young prince's immunity to his pleasing season.
Weeks went by, as he observed from afar,
Seeking signs or hints, a revealing scar.

In the grand library, the truth shone clear,
Books were the prince's hidden, cherished dear.
Seizing the chance, with eyes gleaming in haste,
Rael thought of a book, unmatched in taste.

After a quest, long and profound for a script so unique,
A relic from the past, with a radiant mystique.
Before the prince he stood, the treasure in his hand,
"Dear prince, this rare manuscript is from a far-off land!"

The prince's heart stirred, the allure too strong,
This book in his collection, could right many a wrong.
He agreed, and a deal was struck true,
Rael had triumphed, the prince's Achilles heel he knew.

Moral:

In every stronghold, a vulnerability hides deep,
A soft spot, beneath a facade so steep.
Like Achilles and his exposed heel,
Everyone has a flaw, a chink, a raw feel.

Beneath the armor of a well-crafted soul,
Lies a shadow, often playing a hidden role.
A burning desire, a persistent fear,
Insecurity, or a love one holds dear.

Seek out that weak spot, that delicate glow,
For in its discovery, power can grow.
Use it with care, with art and finesse,
To sway minds, according to your own chess.

But with every move, always be aware,
Exploiting vulnerabilities can lead to despair.
Act with wisdom, and not with spite,
For your own Achilles heel might come to light one night

34. The Peasant and the Dethroned King

In a distant realm, by cruel fate's swing,
Elric, the noble king, saw his reign take a sting.
Ousted from his throne, no army, no land,
He wandered in disguise, avoiding the highland.

Each step, each day, a challenge it became,
Yet his heart stood proud, his spirit aflame.
One day, in a hamlet, weary and devoid of glee,
He knocked on a door, hoping someone would see.

An old welcoming lady, with a soft and gentle grin,
Invited him to her table, sharing her dinner's win.
She gazed at him deeply, seeing his soul's entire length,
"You're no mere peasant, you radiate strength."

The king lowered his eyes, then his sorrow did tell,
"I am Elric," he said, "the king without a crown to dwell."
The old lady smiled, her eyes twinkling like the night,
"You're still a king," she said, "despite your current plight."

In time, Elric, with loyalty by his side,
Reclaimed his kingdom, his lost throne did reside.
For through every ordeal, his stature never did bend,
It's that royal aura that always did defend.

Moral:

If you walk as a king, with a posture so grand,
The world will treat you as a noble in the land.
But if you show vulgarity, lacking sparkle and grace,
You'll be seen as common, with a lost gaze on your face.

The worth we project, to the world outside,
Mirrors back the value, in ourselves we confide.
A king, in his splendor, honors his true essence,
Inspiring in subjects, admiration and reverence.

So, wear your crown, with dignity, without woe,
For the way you present, dictates the respect you'll know.
Show yourself majestic, worthy of praise and song,
And the world will bow, recognizing where you belong.

35. The Farmer and the Seed

In a village nestled among interwoven hills,
Alaric the farmer was revered for his skills.
While neighboring fields in the rain sowed their feed,
His remained barren, not a seed did he lead.

A curious young man approached one fine day,
"Why delay your sowing, Alaric, please say?"
With a gentle smile, Alaric took him aside,
"Nature has its rhythm, its pulse, its tide."

He showed the young man his earth, his land,
How he listened to it, studied its sand.
Patient as dawn, he awaited a sign,
The moment when the soil would truly align.

And when other fields showed pale sight,
Alaric's land was lush, verdant, and bright.
For he knew with patience and gentle care,
Nature offers her bounty, ample and fair.

Moral:

In the dance of time, learn the steps to glide,
Never rush ahead, take moments to reside.
Haste often signals a state of despair,
Keep your composure, success will be there.

Patience is a virtue, in every stance,
Every moment has its time, every chance its dance.
Sense the mood of the time, always stay keen,
For the winds that carry far, and the stars that are seen.

Always be alert, the moment isn't always clear,
But when it finally rings, be ready to draw near.
Strike with precision, with strength and dedication,
Master every instant, that's your true elevation.

36. The King and the Mosquito

In a kingdom with vast horizons wide,
King Lysander shone, his reign undisputed worldwide.
One evening, in deep thought, engrossed and rapt,
A mosquito dared to buzz, to sting, to interrupt.

A guard, seeing the king's frenetic dance,
Offered his swatter, hoping to get a chance.
But the king exclaimed, resolute and strong,
"Why give importance to what doesn't belong?"

The following night, the pest returned again,
But Lysander, unfazed, let it buzz in vain.
The mosquito, weary, sought elsewhere to bite,
A heart less steadfast, more prone to fright.

To his court, the king said, with eyes intense,
"Minor irritations will come, it's common sense,
But do not give them more weight than they should hold,
And you'll see their grip on you quickly fold."

Moral:

To dwell on a worry is to give it a seat,
Pay it too much heed, its power will repeat.
Enemies insignificant, if you believe their lies,
Will grow, take root, and to your surprise.

To rectify a mistake, no matter how slight,
With too much fervor can make the wound ignite.
What you can't grasp, view from a distance high,
Its importance will fade, like a whispering sigh.

For in disregard lies the ultimate might,
To show indifference is to show one's height.
In the face of trifles, always remain calm,
Thus, you'll be in control, holding destiny's palm.

37. The Lustrous Peacock and the Wise Owl

In a distant landscape, the Valley of Shadows lay,
Where every creature, by its image, held sway.
A peacock, named Lustrous, lived in regal glee,
Spreading his feathers, he sought to be the decree.

In this valley, there also was a wise old owl,
Who, in shadows, observed without ever taking a bow.
She knew light could be deceiving and amiss,
Yet, she respected the peacock for his boldness and bliss.

One day, a magical mirror came into sight,
Reflecting reality with no distortion, pure and bright.
Lustrous, wishing to shine, stood before it with pride,
But his reflection showed feathers dull, their brilliance denied.

The owl, approaching softly, whispered in his ear,
"The truth this mirror shows is not to smear.
Appearances may beguile, but are fleeting and transient.
Only what's authentic endures and is persistent."

While the owl, wise and learned,
Spoke of life's truths, as the world turned,
The peacock spread his feathers wide,
Capturing gazes, becoming the pride.

A feast was held, to which all were beckoned,
The owl spoke, but the peacock was the one reckoned.
With shimmering feathers and a song so divine,
He had enchanted every eye, making them shine.

The lesson of the evening was evident and stark,

Present yourself dazzlingly, lighting up the dark,
For the world, when charmed, sees only the flare,
And discreet wisdom often stands back, unaware.

Moral:

In the theater of life, where all's at stake,

Striking images rule, that's the take.

A gesture, a shadow, a powerful sight,

Overshadows the real, and brings the might.

Dazzle the eyes, let the crowd be in awe,

For appearance often dictates the law.

Magnify your shadow, play with the light,

And in the bright glare, your deeds will take flight.

Present yourself in radiant array,

For the charmed world will see only the display.

When image reigns supreme, substance fades away,

True wisdom stays silent, while appearance leads the fray.

38. The Hermit and the Village

In a hamlet, with the gentle scent of rose,
Lived a wise hermit, in retreat, in repose.
On the outskirts of the hustle, at the edge of a grove,
He kept his thoughts, away from the roof and the stove.

One day, a young man, returned from his travels,
With passion and fervor, in the village he unravels.
Of his bright ideas, he spoke incessantly,
Challenging traditions, creating quite a frenzy.

But his passion, his fervor, his pressing verve,
Made the villagers cautious, a bit on the reserve.
They saw him, this stranger, as a great disturbance,
Ready to oust him, without much observance.

The hermit, having heard of the commotion,
Invited the young man, offering gentle devotion.
"Your words carry weight, your heart's in the right place,
But the world, my friend, cannot be hurriedly retrace.

Souls have their fears, their deep-seated ways,
Temper your speech, be gentle, always.
" The young one listened, by the wise one he stayed,
Learned restraint, and his art he displayed.

When he returned to the village, his voice was much softer,
His ideas, though strong, merged like dew on a coffer.
The hamlet, in gratitude, embraced his view,
And thanks to the sage, blossomed anew.

Moral:

In the vast ocean of stirring thoughts so wide,
There is a tide, where some confide.
Think freely, dare to innovate,
But in public, choose to moderate.

For in the crowd, where ideas interlace,
The nonconformist is often the one to face disgrace.
To stand out is to shine, but it's also to dare
Attracting the ire of those who glare.

Display discretion, don't be presumptuous,
Even if inside, a daring flame is continuous.
Share with those, in intimate surround,
Who cherish the unique, and love profound.

In the safety of a kind-hearted circle,
Express your ideas, without the hurdle.
But beyond these walls, where judgments are rife,
Guard your treasures, and keep them in the fife.

39. The Wind and the Mountain

Amid the vast and grand plain,
Stood proudly a mountain, giant and disdain.
Neighboring peaks, in awe of its height,
Admired it, while the wind, envied with spite.

It couldn't move it, despite its fury,
Unlike the dunes it harasses, day and night, in a hurry.
"Oh Mountain!" it cried out boldly one day,
"Facing my force, do you really think you'll stay?"

Then the wind unleashed its wild blow,
Hoping to unsettle this colossus, toe to toe.
But the mountain, against this relentless rage,
Stood firm, unyielding, an unmoving stage.

The wind, cunning, changed its tactic:
Whispers and slander, it became quite didactic.
It tried to erode its base, weaken it bit by bit,
But the mountain remained unshaken, without a hint.

Exhausted, the wind, disappointed, finally ceased,
And the mountain, noble, addressed it, appeased:
"So much effort, Wind, to make me bend,
But you see, my strength is in not yielding to the end."

Moral:

In the arena of conflict, where passions flare,
Keeping calm is the art, the key to the snare.
While the enemy roars, rages and storms,
Stay serene, observe, and find where he deforms.

Look for his weakness, his Achilles' heel,
And with a word, a gesture, watch his fury unreel.
But always keep your mind clear and free,
For it's in calm that solid strategy comes to be.

The advantage goes to one who masters his mind,
Who, despite the storm, finds balance and is kind.
Unsettle the opponent, but remain composed,
For it's this way you'll hold tomorrow, as it's supposed.

40. The King and the Wise Gardener

At the heart of a resplendent kingdom,
The king had a garden so handsome.
But weeds and pests played their part,
Its former glory, from it did depart.

Many gardeners tried their hand,
But all failed, much to the king's despair so grand.
When an old man, with hands worn by age,
Promised to restore the garden's vintage stage.

"What price for this miracle?" The king did ask.
"A high price," the gardener took to the task.
The courtiers laughed, mocking his advanced years,
But the king, intrigued, put aside his fears.

With passion, the wise gardener toiled,
Using rare techniques, skillfully, he coiled.
And behold, the garden amazed every eye,
In all its splendor, it shone again high.

Promise kept, the king paid the fee,
Though for some, it seemed ghostly.
The king declared, head held high, heart so sheer:
"For wisdom, experience, I pay dear."

Moral:

In a world where everything has a cost,

The free, sometimes, raises a doubt embossed.

For what shines without reciprocity,

Often hides a trap or duplicity.

What's valuable deserves its price,

For in paying, one feels so nice.

No debt, no mired chain,

Free from ties, the soul feels no pain.

Bargains and discounts, beware the call,

For excellence and markdown don't align at all.

Pay the fair price, without a frown,

For quality, sometimes, you must be down.

Be generous, but with wisdom so keen,

For prodigality, in excess, can demean.

But spent wisely, with due reason,

It becomes the reflection of a strong season.

41. The Prince and the King's Shadow

In a vast kingdom, a king did shine,
Whose name and deeds were sung in every line.
Upon his death, his natural heir,
Was caught in a storm, living in a shadow's lair.

Each day, each hour, he was compared,
To that legendary father, whose shadow he wearied.
An old counselor, wise and revered, said to him:
"To shine, you must reinvent on a whim."

"Do not build on the same base,
Look elsewhere, create a new pace."
The king decided, not to depart,
But to transform his kingdom, and set himself apart.

He established schools, promoted arts and science,
Invested in the people, valuing every reliance.
He built bridges, connecting cities wide,
And the kingdom flourished, with this new stride.

Years went by, and the once shadowed king,
Now shone bright, a light without a string.
No longer as the son of the past monarch so grand,
But as the ruler who reigned with an innovative hand.

Moral:

Under the first's shine, a shadow may cast,

A brilliant predecessor, hard to outlast.

If into the arena, after them, you tread,

Twice the effort, you'll need to spread.

Do not live in borrowed light,

From a glorious ancestor, or a star out of sight.

For the shadow of the great might consume,

And prevent your own fire from room.

Be not the echo, but the clear voice,

Reject the past, make your own choice.

Slay the giant, rise from its ash,

Shine brightly, be unique, make a splash.

42. The Rotten Apple of the Basket

In a village where all was gay,
Each year, the harvest was celebrated in sway.
But year by year, the luster did wane,
As quarrels and disputes left a stain.

At the heart of yesteryear's festivities,
Whispers and brawls increasingly grew.
The chief, concerned, took careful activities,
And saw Karl, at the center of the ado.

Karl, once loved, had turned bitter,
Envying those who had found success.
Plunging the village into a cold winter,
With rumors, discord, and distress.

The wise chief summoned him aside,
"Change, or from the festivity, you'll be denied."
But Karl, proud, did not yield,
Choosing revolt over the festivity's field.

Without Karl, the festival was pure and fine,
Joy and peace were once again aligned.
The village learned, with a touch of lore,
That one rotten apple can spoil the entire core.

Moral:

Under the sky of a harmonious crew,

There sometimes lurks a foe, not a few.

He whirls, stirs, and disrupts,

And under his weight, the cohesion erupts.

A minion, clothed in pride,

Seeing greatness where only virtue does reside.

If you let him, like a foul wind blow,

He will extinguish the peace's glow.

Do not wait, offer no respite,

For with his hands, he weaves the strike.

He knows neither compromise nor pact,

His game is to sow discord, that's a fact.

Isolate him, remove him from the dance,

Before mistrust takes its chance.

For it's by cutting the rebellious weed,

That the garden regains its natural beauty indeed.

43. The King and the Piper

In a kingdom with far-flung boundaries,
A king ruled, mighty in his tendencies.
Despite his gold, his heavy crown so grand,
The children of the land would not understand.

No shouts, no gold, nor the whip's fear,
Had ever quieted their continuous jeer.
Rowdy and joyful, they would run and play,
Ignoring commands, they'd always stray.

But then one day, a piper came,
With a silver flute, of delicate frame.
"For a gold coin," he said with a grin,
"I'll bring to your children calm from within."

Skeptical yet weary, the king did agree,
The piper played, and magic it came to be.
A gentle melody, like a tender embrace,
Swept through the kingdom, bringing grace.

Enchanted children, under the soothing sound,
Found within them a calm so profound.
The king realized, in a flash of insight,
That heart and soul mattered more than might.

Moral:

In the game of power, strength and might,

Often can crash against a wall so tight.

The key isn't in mere terror or lore,

But in the subtle art of an open door.

Do not use force, or suppression's bind,

For resentment in them will you find.

Seduce the mind, win their heart's confession,

And even the most rebellious will find their own profession.

Every man has his weaknesses, his hidden tales,

Play on his fears, his gentle whims,

And he'll become, without any fails,

A pawn in your hands, as your victory brims.

But neglect the heart, the deep soul's fire,

And hatred will grow, ever higher and higher.

True strength lies in gentleness, not in gear,

Seduce, charm, and harvest happiness, clear.

44. The Thief and the Guard

In a town where night casts its shadows,
A thief thrived, causing many sorrows.
Cunning and elusive, like a breeze so light,
He left behind him, despair and spite.

But a new guard, with a sharp and keen mind,
Came to the town, determined to find
The secret of this thief, the trick of his trade,
To finally catch him, and end the brigade.

He watched the thief's silent entry at night,
His glowing lamp, his evasive flight.
He then mimicked, his gait and his mode,
To play the thief's part, without an episode.

One night, dressed so, he caused an alarm,
Citizens believed they saw the evil do harm.
The thief, intrigued, came to see his reflection,
But fell for the trap, by the guard's direction.

This clever strategist, with his shadowy ruse,
Showed the town that tricks can bemuse,
Where force fails, cunning can prevail,
And wit wins where strength might ail.

Moral:

Before the enemy, play the mirror's part,
Reflections and illusions, to throw off his guard.
Mimic his moves, his gestures, with all your heart,
He'll see himself within, lost and jarred.

For the mirror plays subtle tricks,
Presenting the illusion of shared ethics,
But in reality, it confuses, weakens the fleet,
And the opponent finds himself neatly beat.

In the monkey's dance, there's a lesson so fine,
Humiliate the foe, push him to the line.
Facing the game of reflection, few stand their ground,
And the cunning mirror, brings victory around

45. The Tale of the New King

In a kingdom far and wide,
The king passed away, and the realm sighed.
His son Leon, young and so bold,
Ascended the throne, with a heart full of gold.

He saw hunger, injustice, and deceit,
Dreamed of changing these conditions so bleak.
With great vigor, he announced his view:
Redistribute wealth, and reform anew.

But in his zeal, he moved too fast,
The elites shivered, the populace was aghast.
Nobles in shadows plotted in spree,
While the people doubted what they did see.

A wise man stepped forth, to the king he spoke clear:
"Moderate your steps, or chaos is near.
Change, yes, but with the grace of a dance,
Or you'll lose their trust and the chance for advance."

Heeding these words, Leon changed his pace,
Honored the past, with wisdom and grace.
Each reform, gently, he did lay,
As a bridge between yesterday and today.

Under this new light, tensions did ease,
Love of the people and peace did increase.
For with finesse, he had sailed the wave,
Balancing respect for the past and the change he did crave.

Moral:

When winds of change blow strong and vast,
Don't call for a revolution so fast.
For daily life, bound by routine's tether,
Fears the unknown, the untamed weather.

Step by step, proceed with care,
For haste can stir distrust in the air.
Invoke the past, its light and its might,
While introducing the new, keep history in sight.

The deep roots of ancestral traditions,
Provide strong foundation against harsh conditions.
Change, but softly, without any rout,
For gentle evolution casts the least doubt.

If power is given, play your part well,
Show respect for the past, let it be your spell.
And if you must transform, with boldness or finesse,
Let it be seen as a gentle return, not a fortress.

46. The Tale of Lady Isabella

In a city where roses would bloom,
Lady Isabella, with her grace, lit up the room.
Beauty and talent, knowledge and art,
Each gesture of hers seemed a fresh start.

Though citizens were charmed by her glow,
They found her distant, like a star far below.
Lady Isabella, an icon of unmatched perfection,
Appeared to them a distant reflection.

But at a feast, under candle's gleam,
A cup of wine stained her pristine seam.
All eyes turned, awaiting her reply,
Thinking perfection would be offended, oh my!

But with a laugh, bright, true, and clear,
Isabella admitted to her clumsy stumbles, no fear!
She spoke of falls, of dresses stained,
Times when her grace had completely waned.

From this confession, perceptions turned anew,
Isabella was no longer that goddess they knew.
She was human, with highs and lows in store,
And in every heart, her image did soar.

Now, admired from every view,
Lady Isabella was deeply loved, it's true.
For showing one's flaws means opening your core,
And true perfection touches souls evermore.

Moral:

In the world's shimmer where everyone seeks to shine,
Perfection allures but can also confine.
Too much brilliance awakens envy's shade,
For no one wants to feel their glow fade.

A step too perfect, a flawless smile,
Can weave around you a darkened file.
Jealousy lurks, silent and sly,
Ready to drag you into its quiet sky.

So, show now and then, a flaw, a scar,
It extinguishes many a whispering star.
Admit, without shame, a folly or vice,
Humanity loves to see a soul not precise.

Being human means admitting a weakness,
In our imperfections, there's born a uniqueness.
So, don't always aim to stand atop a high ledge,
For only gods and the dead never edge.

47. The Tale of King Aleron

In the heart of a vast kingdom shone Aleron,
A king with ambitions stretching beyond the dawn.
Every land conquered, every city tamed,
Made him prouder, fueling his proclaimed fame.

After a victory on a golden land,
He decreed that a celebration would stand.
Feasts and tournaments, the joy prolonged,
But triumph's intoxication his heart wronged.

Before the jubilant crowd, he did state,
To take the stronger lands, without wait.
But his wise advisors, whispering by his side,
Tried to temper his unmatched pride.

"O king," they said, "these lands are feared,
With strong armies, firmly geared."
But Aleron, in his pride, brushed their words aside,
Launching the assault, new trophies on his mind.

But neighboring kings, united in an alliance,
Against Aleron, showed their defiance.
Defeated, captured, his fate became clear,
Not by death, but by exile, he'd disappear.

On a distant island, alone he'd stay,
Regretting his mistakes, in silence he'd sway.
The once powerful king, fallen from his stage,
Learned that unchecked ambition leads to cage.

Moral:

In the glow of a blazing win,

Silent dangers often begin.

The euphoria of triumph, intense and fleeting,

Can blind us, our path depleting.

With a heart swollen with newfound might,

The desire to conquer more sights is right,

But overreaching, aiming too high,

Can cast shadows, and misfortunes amplify.

For excess in all leads to stray,

Too much success can lead our way.

Enemies will rise, more numerous, more fierce,

If, in intoxication, caution we pierce.

Victory is sweet, but should not intoxicate,

Stay humble and wise, always contemplate.

Plan with care, strategy in mind,

For only the wise know when to draw the line.

48. The River and the Mountain

In the heart of a valley, proud Mount Ergo stood tall,
An unchanging giant, casting a shadow over all.
Steadfast, strong, defying the seasons' sway,
It watched, timeless, scanning the horizon each day.

In its crevices, Serpens gently wound,
Glistening in the sun, it danced all around.
Never stagnant, always in flow,
Bringing life, it followed where the currents would go.

An earthquake shook the ground, the valley stirred,
Ergo trembled, its attire got blurred.
Its stones blocked the stream, Serpens found itself trapped,
But the water, rebellious, looked and found its way mapped.

Over centuries, with patience, it carved its mark,
Wearing down the mountain's base, showing its spark.
From the massive mountain, valleys and hills emerged,
Showing that with time, even the solid gets purged.

Moral:

In a world of change, don't be like stone,

For rigidity can lead to downfall, all alone.

Avoid set plans, and paths too straight,

For challenges lurk, ready to dictate your fate.

Be like the shimmering water, elusive and swift,

Changing, adapting, always ready to lift.

In uncertainties, remain alert, always aware,

Don't await the rule, but follow your own solar flare.

For everything in this world is in a constant dance,

Seasons, tides, life, and every chance.

Guard yourself by being in eternal motion,

Know that everything changes, like waves in the ocean.

49. The King and the Council Birds

In a realm far away, under a fortress's shade,
A king, with heart so proud, sat as a bird of great parade.
At the break of day, two birds to him would commence:
The Nightingale voiced truths with great persistence.

While the Peacock, with unmatched brilliance,
Praised endlessly, with royal sycophance.
"O King," he proclaimed, "you're the moon and the sun,
Your glory shines bright, second to none."

The Nightingale, gently, tried to forewarn,
Of storms on the horizon, of sorrows unborn.
"My King," he said, "beyond your golden walls,
Shadows grow, and desolate are the calls."

The king, wearied by these bitter reports,
Banished the Nightingale, keeping the sincere cohorts.
But without the Nightingale to guide his hand,
His kingdom faltered, entering a decline so grand.

Moral:

Better a frank word, though harsh to the ear,

Than empty flattery that drifts you from what's clear.

Always seek to surround yourself with truth,

For it's loyalty that builds true prosperity, in sooth.

Better to hear a truth that hurts but awakens,

Than a sweet illusion that sneakily partakes.

Flattery may charm, but it's a fleeting candle's glare,

While honesty, though stern, is a genuine light to bear.

Surround yourself with those who dare speak without pretense,

For in loyalty, one can paint a foundation dense.

True prosperity isn't just in goods or gold,

But in the honesty of bonds, time and time again retold.

50. The Lion, the Oxen, and the Meadows

In the heart of the savannah, under a scorching sun,
The king lion, watched, biding his time, none to shun.
Three strong and valiant oxen grazed side by side,
And by their unity, all dangers they'd deride.

With every attempt, the lion was driven away,
For united, they stood, none could make them sway.
But the clever king saw beyond the moment's frame,
He knew the key lay in sowing seeds of blame.

He whispered praises into the first ox's ear,
Telling him he was stronger, deserving of cheer.
To the second, he spoke of envy and betrayal,
And to the third, he hinted at a power play so frail.

Little by little, the oxen, once brothers of the field,
Became divided, harboring resentment, their bond did yield.
Separated, each felt stronger in his own space,
Oblivious that they'd become prey in this chase.

The cunning lion approached without any delay,
Feasted on the first, the second couldn't get away.
And the third, alone, with no ally by his side,
Realized too late that together they could've defied.

Moral:

Together, it's said, mountains we can move,
Unity is strength, as countless tales prove.
Yet, in the shadows, some play a different game,
Seeking to divide, to ignite a divisive flame.

The age-old maxim, "divide and conquer" stands true,
Not just a saying, but a weapon to subdue.
For against a united front, power may waver,
But against divided troops, it'll savor its flavor.

Whether aiming for a throne or a simple crown,
The strategy remains: separate, and the world bows down.
Remember, by sowing discord you might gain station,
For division, after all, strengthens your foundation.

51. King Cleon and the Ever-Present Shadow

In a vast kingdom, a king named Cleon reigned,
Feared and revered, his power never waned.
Though rarely seen in public view,
His presence was felt, like a mystical spell it drew.

Tales said he had eyes everywhere to look,
Each bird or stone was his spy, his rook.
Every whisper, every secret, every deceit,
Was known to the king, making his legend complete.

Nobles, not wanting to displease Cleon's gaze,
Avoided plots and betrayals, always cautious in their ways.
The people, believing in their king's foresight,
Lived in peace, trusting his might.

But in truth, Cleon had merely sown,
Hints and rumors that had everyone overthrown.
Without truly being everywhere, he managed to instill,
Fear and respect, without ever having to kill.

Moral:

The impression of omnipresence is a tool of rule,
Warding off threats, making hope the jewel.
For even if one cannot see and know all,
The illusion alone establishes the protocol.

When it's believed your eyes can be anywhere cast,
That every whisper, every secret, you can grasp,
Influence grows, and respect is earned fast,
Even if omnipresence is but a deceptive broadcast.

The shadow of your presence hovers, making all wary,
Deterring plots and strengthening loyalty in a hurry.
For in power, the art of illusion is golden,
Appearing to be is as strong as being, when well beholden.

52. The Oak and the Willow

In the heart of a lush and bright forest,
Stood an oak, proud, strong, and earnest.
Beside it danced a willow, flexible, filled with glee,
Changing with the wind, forever free.

The oak, standing firm, faced every storm,
A symbol of might, it was the norm.
But the willow, with grace, would bend and adjust,
Each gust strengthened it, breaking it was a nonplus.

One night, the wind howled, carrying all away,
By morning, the oak on the ground lay.
The willow, despite its dances and turns,
Stood tall, ready for whatever returns.

Moral:

To adapt is like dancing with the breeze,

But in your heart, always keep your peace.

Facing the tides of time, know how to evolve,

Is to embrace change without ever dissolving.

The world moves, whirls, and shifts,

In face of this dance, maintain your uplifts.

Yet, stay open, curious, and aware,

For true strength lies in balance, rare.

Each challenge, every worry, every test,

Is an opportunity to show your best, your zest.

In the hurricane of change, remain grounded,

But like the reed, know when to be rounded.

53. Epilogue : To the Loyal Readers

Through the fables of power, you've followed step by step,
Through morals and lessons, navigating every misstep.
Thank you for listening to tales of times long ago,
Each rule, each moral, each subtle tip-toe.

Dear readers, your journey doesn't end here,
For a new adventure soon draws near.
A second volume is in the works for you,
For a dive into a world thrilling and new.

In this era where digital reigns supreme,
Where pixels and data flow like a stream,
I offer you a glimpse into a world anew,
Where La Fontaine and technology intertwine and ensue.

"**Fables 2.0: La Fontaine in the Digital Age**" will be the name,
Of animals, of pixels, in a sequel to acclaim.
A world where the old and the modern blend,
Where timeless stories meet the era's trend.

The dog gets lost in his touchscreen device,
While the eagle converses with a drone so precise.
The cricket shares her song on YouTube for fun,
The fox, on social media, gives everyone a run.

So, let your curiosity be sparked, fanned,
For this new odyssey is close at hand.
Expect lessons that are revamped, modernized,
Where the past and future are harmonized.

www.ingramcontent.com/pod-product-compliance
Lightning Source LLC
LaVergne TN
LVHW051923160726
843515LV00002B/14

* 9 7 8 2 8 9 8 6 4 0 0 7 0 *